therapists, with their sophisticated behavior plans, have created more unwanted behaviors than benefits. *Autism Breakthrough* provides common-sense approaches on how to establish harmonious, humanistic relationships based on trust and unconditional allowance and acceptance. *Autism Breakthrough* is a successful guide to empower people on the autism spectrum to relate and thrive in our day-to-day world, and a significant contribution to the awakening of humanity to neurodiversity."

—Ken Routson, author of *The Gifts of Autism & Alzheimer's* and *Beliefology*

"*Autism Breakthrough* truly breaks through the 'autism is a lifelong condition' paradigm and shifts hopelessness to hope. As occupational therapists and international lecturers, we will be highly recommending this wonderful 'user-friendly' resource with all the principles, strategies, and techniques needed to support children and adults with social-relational challenges."

—MarySue Williams and Sherry Shellenberger, creators of the Alert Program® and authors of Alert Program® books, games, and trainings

"Insightful, personal, and accessible. A hopeful message, and one which only a person that has looked through the eyes of an autistic child could offer. *Autism Breakthrough* is a must-read for all parents of special children. Its depth will touch you and the practical advice will empower you to join your child on their journey toward achieving their unique and limitless potential."

—Alex Doman, coauthor of *Healing at the Speed of Sound* and founder and CEO of Advanced Brain Technologies, creators of The Listening Program®